THE TALE OF MAC & MURPHY

THE MOST IMPORTANT BUSINESS DECISION YOU'LL EVER MAKE

DAVID WAYNE WIMER

CONTENTS

First Edition

Although the author and publisher have made every effort to ensure that the information in this book was correct at press time, the author and publisher do not assume and hereby disclaim any liability to any party for any loss, damage, or disruption caused by errors or omissions, whether such errors or omissions result from negligence, accident, or any other cause.

This is a work of fiction. Unless otherwise indicated, all the names, characters, businesses, places, events, and incidents in this book are either the product of the author's imagination or used in a fictitious manner. Any resemblance to actual persons, living or dead, or actual events is purely coincidental.

Published by David Wimer Advisors, LLC
E: author@davidwimer.com

Manufactured & Produced in the United States of America

Paperback ISBN: 979-8-9859815-0-6
eBook ISBN: 979-8-9859815-1-3

David Wimer Advisors, LLC, Reading, PA

Per Angusta ad Augusta
[*Through Trials to Triumph*]

To the business owners I've served and learned from over the years, my former partners at Murphy McCormack, and to my son Eric, a passionate and gifted entrepreneur.

— David Wayne Wimer

PROLOGUE: THE CASE FOR READINESS

This book is for privately held, family business owners. I wrote this tale to share what I learned about the single most important decision you face in your business (with a nod to Shakespeare): to Value-Prep, or not to Value-Prep. Choose to confront it now or choose to ignore it. When value-prep has been confronted early in a business' life cycle, you may end up looking like a genius down the road, without having to do anything special. The consequences of ignoring it, on the other hand, can be devastating to you and those you love.

Procrastinators say they'll get around to it and ultimately decide, "It's better to be lucky than to be good." Risk takers by nature, owners and entrepreneurs may not heed words of caution. Unfortunately for them, it may become too late to make this critical decision. As for naysayers and non-believers alike, I have seen case after case where this one decision determined the difference between an abundant or meager future. Fifty percent of business owners will involuntarily sell or transfer a business because of a sudden event thrust upon them (death, divorce, disability, distress, or disagreement). For all we do control, this one decision influences the amount of wealth you've worked so hard to build in your business.

Timing is almost never convenient: the odds may also not be in your favor at a moment when you need high value the most. After investing countless hours, years, capital, and personal energy into your business, you may be left with nothing to show for it but debt and liabilities. You may have lost the income stream and the lifestyle you enjoy. I assure you, if you choose to use Value as a measurement of business success, being in a constant state of readiness will protect this asset you've worked so hard to build. You can build financial strategies that work for you and carry you to those achievements of which you've always dreamed. It only takes a little time to gain a lot of clarity.

When we begin the story of our two fictional business owners, Murphy is faced with a looming catastrophe. Using his cousin Mac as a sounding board, Murphy searches for answers and accepts the help of a referred, trusted Value Advisor. Enjoy the magical journey of Murphy's transformation and how he faces the single most important decision he'll ever make in his business.

Are you ready?

David Wayne Wimer

CHAPTER ONE

MAC & MURPHY

"How we act is who we become."

Mac & Murphy were business owners in the small town of Donegal, Ohio. Not only that, they were also cousins. Mac owned Mac Inc., a regional distributor of specialty metals for aerospace and medical applications. Murphy owned Murphy & Co., a Northeast US distributor of seasonal holiday decorations and related services. Their fathers were business owners, as were their grandfathers, and every generation before. Their family had first arrived by packet ship from Ireland in the early 1800's. It was a family legacy that kept them close-knit. But trouble was brewing that could break this long string of ownership.

A global pandemic (imagine that) had occurred, and panic was setting into the business community across America and the globe. It was almost as bad as the Great Depression (at least in Murphy's mind). This unknown and invisible disease threatened not only lifestyles, but life itself. Not seen in over 100 years since the Spanish Flu, it looked like both businesses could be in jeopardy with the possibility that one business may fail, and one business may survive. How awful that thought was to Murphy and Mac! How devastating this news would be to the entire family!

Murphy was such an intelligent, hard-working, kind, and generous fellow with a family of four children, just like Mac. The family also knew that Murphy was a pessimist, highly unusual for any of their family members. That dose of pessimism helped keep Murphy in business for many, many years. His favorite saying followed (you guessed it) Murphy's Law, *"If something can go wrong, it usually will."* That mindset allowed Murphy to get through some difficult years in business.

Murphy seemed resolved that this was destiny, out of his control. Just last month he ordered enough goods to get him through the holiday season, when the bad news came by email. The manufacturers of his exclusive distribution contracts were shutting down across the globe. And there was a potential that he would not have holiday seasonal items for his customers. Murphy was very troubled about the news. With something so terrifying and destructive, Murphy did not know what to do. So, like he did with family crises, he called his cousin Mac.

CHAPTER TWO

COUSIN MAC'S CALL

"Curiosity has been my greatest teacher."

Mac was a curious guy and had been in business just as long as Murphy. He enjoyed having a family of four and spent quality time with them. He worked hard, sacrificing long hours to provide the best he could. Mac was also involved in his community and could be counted on to share time, talent, and treasure with others. He was active in his Church and had developed a strong faith. Most importantly, he had a quiet confidence in his abilities to figure out any situation that was thrust upon him. Murphy knew Mac was always a pillar of optimism and confidence, especially in a business crisis, which he figured was due to Mac being unusually resourceful or plain lucky.

Mac would always say, "If things go wrong, and one is prepared, there are always options." You have to love his optimism, which contrasted sharply with his cousin Murphy, the Pessimist's philosophy.

No one wants to hear the news that something they've been dreading has come to pass. The bagel shop was sold out of cream cheese so we couldn't enjoy our favorite breakfast, or the grocery shelves were empty of laundry detergent and the dirty clothes were piling up at home. Well, imagine this call between Murphy and Mac! This was much bigger than cream cheese and laundry detergent! With everything they owned at stake, a situation beyond Mac & Murphy's control was about to impact one of their lives substantially.

This situation warranted more than a text, an email, or a Facebook message. This kind of call was reserved for the most intensive and potentially time-consuming situation imaginable. It was reserved for use only in times of death, divorce, disability, distress, or disagreement as the cousins had agreed upon since the advent of texting. Therefore, Murphy picked up his phone and FaceTimed his cousin Mac. Things were about to get very distressing.

"Hey, Mac!" said Murphy. "How are you and the family doing?"

Mac responded, "We are doing well, Murphy, in spite of my recent surgery."

"I saw your text a month ago and the pics on Facebook of you leaving the hospital," said Murphy. "The wheelchair ride must have been uncomfortable. You were grimacing. How's your recuperation, Mac?"

Mac told Murphy all about his operation. The surgeon told him he needed to lose 30 pounds before surgery so Mac would recuperate quicker and would put less stress on his new knees.

"Knees?" Murphy said.

"Yes, knees. I had both knees operated on at the same time."

"Wow! That's a big risk, isn't it?" Murphy questioned.

"Yes, it can be," said Mac. "I had to diet and exercise for nine months prior to surgery. I even took extra supplements and kept track of my blood pressure and glucose readings in a diary."

"That seems like a lot of work," said Murphy.

"It was, and it wasn't," replied Mac. "There was no possibility of the surgery without preparing myself for it."

Murphy sighed. He couldn't imagine taking nine months to prepare for surgery. There was more than enough work to do at the office and at home with the kids in sports. Community work would certainly have suffered. Murphy was getting depressed thinking about all that work distracting him from his business. How in the world did Mac do it? That thought would stay with Murphy for a while.

"Hey, Murphy, it's good to hear from you. Is everything all right with your family? Did you hear about this global pandemic?" asked Mac.

Murphy took a deep breath and sighed once more, "Everyone is healthy. We're stocking up on toilet paper and paper towels and hand sanitizer right now. We expect to be using lots of it. And we're worried about being able to get staples at the grocery stores. Boy, who would have imagined that hand sanitizer would be so popular? Should have been in that business."

"Why do you say that, Murphy? Is there something you wanted to talk about with your business?" asked Mac. Murphy looked down for a moment like he had lost his best friend. Mac had read his mind, seeing how they were close cousins.

Murphy replied, "Well, as a matter-of-fact, Mac, I do want to share something with you. I know I can trust you to keep it confidential. I just received an email from my largest manufacturer overseas and they notified me that they were shutting down production. Within hours I received the same kind of apology note from all my manufacturers. That means we won't have goods for the holiday season. And that will be devastating to my business. No shipments. No goods. And no income."

Mac couldn't help but feel the pain in Murphy's voice. Murphy had invested his life in his business to provide for his family. He knew Murphy earned an above average income and lived in a nice suburban development in a wonderful school district where his kids participated in plenty of after-school extracurriculars and sports. He also knew Murphy was very generous to his employees when they were in need, almost to a fault. He would help by giving them extra hours at his distribution center, even when there wasn't much to do. Murphy was a giver.

As a business owner, Murphy had been methodical about building up his above average lifestyle. He even survived the Great Depression of 2007-2009. That meant a lot in business owner circles at his country club. His goods were in demand during that financial upheaval as they made people feel happy during the holiday season. This situation now seemed altogether different. Mac couldn't help but wonder how Murphy had gotten boxed into this corner.

Murphy suddenly said to Mac, "Hey, Mac, I have a call from my banker coming in that I must take. May I call you back after that call?" Mac agreed. As he signed off, he told Murphy to let him sleep on it overnight before talking again. Mac always believed in the power of his unconscious to solve problems while he got a good night's rest. Ironically, he knew Murphy's night may be fitful.

"Sure thing," said Mac. "I'm around tomorrow. Just Face-Time me when it's good for you." The two agreed and hung up on what would be the first call of several calls to come.

CHAPTER THREE

THE BANKER'S CALL

"Trust is offered to all, until proven otherwise."

Murphy's banker had called him as the news about international travel, overseas manufacturing production, supply chain constraints and potential effects of the global health crisis hit the Financial Times. Journalists on their business beats for the news media were seeking answers, interviewing health officials all around the globe. No one really knew much, other than that people were becoming ill, and many were hospitalized. The medical community was in a heightened state of emergency as the disease spread quickly and hospital beds were in demand. This was the backdrop for Murphy's call.

Murphy had a great banking relationship with his banker, Liam, also a fellow country club member. Liam had financed Murphy for many years, enjoying his company's solid growth and earnings. He knew Murphy's outlook was conservative and that Murphy was a realist, which at times could be misinterpreted as pessimistic. Murphy was known to sandbag at golf, and he always would under-promise and over-deliver in business.

Liam had been encouraging Murphy to get some outside help to assess his business and strategy for growth, as he employed over 30 people. But Murphy was always reluctant to act on that suggestion. Murphy was a very private and proud business owner who had navigated the business through several recessions. He also knew Murphy had survived the Great Recession of 2007-2009 and unlike some of his peers, did not have investments in assets like rental real estate or travel & hospitality. Nor did he hold investment stocks like Bear Stearns or AIG that had tanked during that time. Because of his past, Liam naturally gave Murphy the benefit of the doubt when it came to operating his business.

"Hi, Liam," Murphy said as he picked up the phone. "What can I do for you?"

Liam replied, "I just wanted to check in on you to see how you and your family were doing with this health crisis. Is everyone healthy?"

Murphy said, "That's very thoughtful, Liam. Yes, everyone seems to be doing fine. Other than we needed to build more shelves in the basement to store all the toilet paper, paper towels and hand sanitizer."

Both men chuckled at this as Liam had experienced the same thing at home. "Is everything ok with business?" Liam asked.

Murphy hesitated for a second and said, "It's too early to say. We are sorting through communications from overseas, but nothing has been confirmed. It seems everyone is trying to understand what we are dealing with, and our suppliers are no different overseas than they are here in the United States." *All true*, thought Murphy as he felt relief in saying that to Liam. He just did not want to set off a red flag with him when he didn't really know the extent of the crisis. Perhaps it would be a couple weeks and things would settle down.

Liam responded positively, "Well Murphy, if anyone knows what to do in a crisis, I'm sure you already have a plan. Stay healthy." With that Liam wished Murphy a good day and hung up.

As Murphy hung up, he had a sinking feeling in his stomach. It felt as bad as the white lie he had told his seventh-grade nun in parochial school, when he denied joining some classmates in sipping the wine stored in the sacristy for Mass. Murphy had learned from being exonerated then, that it's better to tell a partial truth than an outright lie. And Liam was no exception. Murphy needed more information before he could say anything to Liam. And he would start to get some answers firsthand over the next week.

CHAPTER FOUR

THE SUPPLIERS' CALL

*"Our imagination is a powerful tool. We can use it to create
new possibilities, or to magnify fears and doubt."*

The next day, the news Murphy's suppliers shared one after the
other nearly gave Murphy ulcers. How could this be happening?
It seemed the whole world was in a tailspin. Internally,
Murphy's sales force became alarmed by the backlog of unfilled
orders. They instantly knew what that meant to them as
commissioned salespeople: payment delays and low earnings.
The customer care and logistics departments began to receive
inquiries about customer orders. Not knowing what the extent
or duration of the crisis would be, customers were reassured
that Murphy himself was on top of it. That seemed to relieve
some of the pressure. However, as the week went along,
everyone could see Murphy's pessimism grow.

Customers were calling about order and deposit status to

understand if either were in jeopardy. Murphy became agitated easily when he did not have adequate answers for customers. As best he could, Murphy told the partial story of his calls overseas to verify status, which alleviated his discomfort. What he didn't say though, was even more important, in that he was still in the dark about timing and fulfillment of their orders. He had no solid answers for his employees or customers. Murphy realized he was in denial, but this was how he had gotten through difficulties in the past. Hold bad news close to the vest and eventually he would figure out a solution. It had always turned out fine in the long run. Murphy knew if he needed help to overcome feelings of hopelessness, he could seek counsel from his doctor. Lately his blood pressure was higher than normal and that also irritated him.

Before the week ended, Murphy received a call from the major supplier of fifty percent of his goods. The supplier told Murphy there could be a delay until they could return the plant to normal to produce the goods Murphy expected for the season. He was told not to count on receiving much for this holiday season. Shipments were at a standstill due to lack of production. More frustrating than that: all of his deposits would be kept on account on their books until the crisis was over. Murphy became angry at the prospect of the manufacturer holding his deposits. The supplier knew how important customers in the United States counted on Murphy and his company. Murphy wasn't very understanding. The thought of having to relay this to Liam was overwhelming.

Murphy remembered he was supposed to return the call to his cousin Mac the next day for his insights, but the week had gotten away from him. Murphy ruminated about his situation and grew more pessimistic with each day that week. There were no immediate solutions. No thoughts of strategy. And worse than that, although he knew he had a large line of credit for working capital, without billings, he would eventually be constrained to make payroll. Murphy needed to call Mac at once to hammer out a solution.

CHAPTER FIVE

THE SECOND CALL TO MAC

"Unseen forces are at work in every situation we face."

Murphy called Mac late on Friday afternoon near closing time so he and Mac could talk after hours. Mac accepted his FaceTime request and saw that Murphy was stressed. In fact, Murphy dispensed with any familiar chit-chat and dove right into his problem. After several minutes of non-stop venting to Mac about his difficult week, Murphy asked, "So what do you think I should do about Liam and my suppliers?"

Mac saw his cousin was irritated. He had never seen Murphy this way. Mac was careful to listen, concentrating on Murphy's discomposure first. Mac replied, "Tell me how you've been feeling, Murphy." Murphy melted. It was the first time lately that anyone had asked him about his emotional health. Murphy was quite good at keeping his work difficulties from his wife, Mary, and his children.

Murphy replied, "To tell you the truth, I have not been

feeling like myself lately. This situation has stressed me out more than any other time I've been in business. I'm afraid I'll be the first in our lineage to go out of business. And that scares me the most."

Mac responded, "That's understandable, Murphy. From what you just told me, your company is in a real pickle."

Murphy went on, "Yeah, and I just don't know what to tell my banker, Mac. We have a million-dollar line of credit and I'm afraid if he finds out my supplier situation, he will reduce his exposure or ask for more collateral. I'm not lying to him. I'd rather tell him part of the truth than the whole truth."

"That must be difficult," Mac replied.

Mac gently asked Murphy for permission to ask a few more questions to help understand his situation before moving on. With Murphy's acknowledgement, Mac continued, "Hey, Murphy, have you ever had someone come in and assess your business situation? Perhaps there are some things that an independent, objective person can suggest? Maybe there's something they've learned in other business situations that can be applied to yours. Or maybe there are hidden solutions that can be uncovered." Murphy was silent for a few moments. He knew what Mac meant. Mac wasn't the first person to suggest it. Over the years, Liam also broached the subject.

Murphy knew he had been too stubborn and set in his ways, not open-minded to allowing someone else to assist him. He felt uncomfortable with the concept of letting an outsider into his thoughts, feelings, and business matters. Why should he? He had always been able to solve things himself. Occasionally, he'd gotten ideas from Conor, his CPA but those were only tax related, not income related. Mostly he got ideas after golf at the country club over a few cocktails from his buddies. He was comfortable with these other business owners. No one really got into anything deep or difficult. And everyone seemed happy, successful and in control. He oftentimes picked up a kernel of wisdom learning how they did this or that in their businesses. Murphy listened to what worked and didn't work for them. But that was it. Engaging an advisor sounded so formal, like giving up with no solutions. It was an undeniable statement that he needed help. He didn't want to appear vulnerable, especially to his golfing foursome. Now Murphy was more conflicted than ever before.

Murphy replied, "Well, Mac, is that the best you can do?"

Mac replied, "Murphy, I've watched you suffer with this situation and realize it must be weighing heavily on your mind day and night. If it were me, it would keep me awake at nights and I'd be miserable too. After reflecting on your situation, it's apparent to me you could use some insight. I'm busy enough with my business and this crisis so I'm not your answer. Like your golf buddies, the advice I took a while ago may not work in your situation. I don't want to do more harm than good. I know each business is unique. Providing a prescription for a problem in a crisis, without understanding the correct diagnosis, well, that's just a formula for malpractice." Murphy listened intently. Mac went on, "Talking with someone may help you gain insights and options, Murphy. Of course, there's no guarantee. But the size and scope of your business problem dictate that you apply the best resources available towards a solution, correct?"

Murphy reluctantly agreed, "Yeah, I suppose you are right."

Mac went on, "I'll email you the number of someone I've used in the past who helped me. Let me know what you think after you've talked with her." With that, Murphy thanked Mac and said he'd look forward to receiving his referral. Murphy was still feeling anxious. He was conflicted about using an outside advisor. Agreeing to follow through on Mac's suggestion to call the advisor provided some minor relief. Murphy knew he was in a "pickle" as Mac described it. He had a glimmer of hope that the next day would help him start resolving his high level of stress and worry.

CHAPTER SIX

THE REFERRAL

"Many times, the real opponent is resistance from within."

Murphy received an email early Monday with Mac's referral, an advisor named Ms. Rahbull. Murphy looked at the email skeptically. He had never heard of this person. She didn't have a first name. But there was a faint familiarity in her name, he just couldn't put his finger on it as he scratched his chin.

Am I supposed to call this woman, Ms. Rahbull? he wondered. The voice in his head started to warn him, *What can she know that I don't know?* He had heard many stories about so-called business advisors who had bilked people by posing as experts. Thank goodness he had never succumbed to such a sales pitch. Nevertheless, he was in a great deal of stress, worry and confusion. He respected his cousin Mac as a businessman and trusted his suggestion as a concerned family member. Murphy thought no longer, touched his phone keypad, and dialed her number.

The call was answered by a very pleasant, voice-recorded

auto attendant. It said, "Thank you for your call. I want to prioritize your call back. Please press #1 if you are an existing client, leave your name and number and I will call you back within 24 hours. If you are not a client, and this is an emergency, please press #2, leave the nature of your emergency, and I will call you back within 10 minutes. Thank you and I look forward to talking with you soon." Murphy pressed #2, left his name and number and said he had an overseas major supplier issue that was going to devastate his business, and that he was referred by his cousin Mac. He had not heard anyone ever prioritize their callbacks like this in business. He wondered how Ms. Rahbull had trained customers to accept call backs in 24 hours? Well, he would find out more when she called him back.

Within 9 minutes and 52 seconds, Murphy received a call back, but to his disappointment, it was not from Ms. Rahbull, but rather from one of her assistants, Mr. Hastie. Murphy thought, *That's a funny name.* Mr. Hastie said that Ms. Rahbull would be delayed due to assisting a potential client like him who had an emergency, and that she would like to understand what led up to this emergency call, so she could be helpful when she was free to call him back. Mr. Hastie asked if he could record Murphy's call and Murphy quickly agreed. Murphy wanted Ms. Rahbull to understand his story firsthand. Murphy had his story well-prepared in his head and proceeded to take ten minutes of Mr. Hastie's time to explain it all in detail. Mr. Hastie listened intently and never interrupted. As Murphy talked, he also heard Mr. Hastie vigorously typing in the background. At the end of the call, Mr. Hastie thanked him and assured him that Ms. Rahbull would be back to him as soon as possible. Murphy ended the call and hoped he would hear something soon.

CHAPTER SEVEN
THE THIRD CALL TO MAC

"When we transcend discomfort with hope as our ally,
we become comfortable being uncomfortable."

Murphy was concerned that Ms. Rahbull would not call him back and that Mac may have steered him wrong. He wanted reassurance by talking with Mac again, so he called him. "How are you, Murphy?" said Mac when he answered his phone. "Have you had an opportunity to talk with Ms. Rahbull?" Murphy explained his experience with leaving a message, and the call from Mr. Hastie. Mac asked, "Was your call returned within ten minutes?" Murphy acknowledged it was nine minutes and 52 seconds. Mac asked, "Did you speak with Ms. Rahbull?" Murphy said he didn't and that he was disappointed a Mr. Hastie had called him back.

Mac chuckled. Murphy didn't think this was so funny, especially since Mac knew Murphy was having an emergency. Mac sensed Murphy's sensitivity and apologized. "I'm sorry,

Murphy, but Ms. Rahbull deals with emergencies every day. In fact, I was one of those emergency calls when I first called her way back when." Murphy couldn't believe what Mac was admitting. Murphy had always thought Mac just applied his optimism to get through any business issue he confronted. Mac's revelation that he had once needed Ms. Rahbull tempered Murphy's irritation with him. "I may have forgotten to tell you she never is the first one to call you back in 10 minutes. But it's always nice to get a call back in an emergency in 10 minutes, isn't it? You understand now why she employed Mr. Hastie. Don't be angry with Mr. Hastie as he's very efficient at his job. And so is Ms. Rahbull."

Murphy grumbled, "Some system for setting expectations. Will I get a chance to talk to Ms. Rahbull?"

Mac said, "You can count on it."

With that, Murphy said, "I certainly hope so." The call ended with Mac telling Murphy it will be well worth the wait.

CHAPTER EIGHT
MS. RAHBULL

"We are accountable for our emotions when thoughts
pilot them without a compass."

The phone rang the next day just as Mac had indicated. A sweet and kind voice asked, "Hello, is this Murphy?"

Murphy immediately stopped shuffling papers on his desk and responded, "Yes, this is Murphy. Who is this?"

Ms. Rahbull answered, "This is Ms. Rahbull, and I am returning your call. I understand from my associate, Mr. Hastie, that you have a business in distress and are looking for some assistance. Is that correct?"

"You are spot on!" said Murphy. He liked how this conversation had started.

"Well then, if you would tell me this first, were you ready for something like this to happen?"

Murphy couldn't help himself. "Ms. Rahbull, with all due

respect, I need help now. Asking me silly questions, like being ready for a catastrophe, isn't going to get me out of this mess."

Ms. Rahbull in her kind and sweet voice replied, "I understand your skepticism, Murphy. And I did not mean to upset you. I asked that question to understand your philosophy about business. What did you do in the past to get through tough times?"

Murphy thought for a minute and responded, "Well...I... learned how to work around things that happened. My way has always worked. But this is a catastrophe of gigantic proportions, unlike anything I've never seen before."

With that, Ms. Rahbull asked, "So, what did those situations teach you?"

Murphy was perplexed. He hadn't thought about learning anything. He just knew he was lucky to get through industry downturns and economic upheavals like the Great Recession, and that now he was facing something awful again. He dearly wanted to just get on with her solving his problem. The only thing that came to mind was his outlook on life in general, "If you must know, I can tell you easily," he said. *"If something can go wrong, it usually will."*

Murphy immediately felt a bit awkward for telling her his view. Why? He had only revealed that to a few trusted people like his golf buddies, Mac, and Conor. What was happening to him here, he thought? Murphy started to feel uncomfortable. Why was this person asking him about his philosophy in business?

There was a silent pause in the conversation before Ms. Rahbull spoke. "Murphy, given that outlook and the problem you face the size of a fire-breathing dragon, I think we can work together to help you." Murphy suddenly felt relieved. Maybe this would be his answer to his prayers. He was having so much stress these days he hardly enjoyed his favorite calf's head soup, and corned beef and cabbage last night.

Then he asked the golden question: "Before I consent to working with you, Ms. Rahbull, do you have any references?"

Ms. Rahbull answered politely and with the sweetest voice, "All of my clients are private people, like you, who have engaged us to help in a crisis or to prevent a business catastrophe. No one likes to look back and relive painful moments in their business. Most just move on when they have learned what to do." Murphy listened carefully. "Like a doctor, I am sworn to an oath of confidentiality. So, I'm sorry I am unable to help you if you need more than a trusted referral." said Ms. Rahbull.

"No! No! Ms. Rahbull. It's not necessary, I was just asking." blurted Murphy. Sweat started to form on his brow. Then he asked the question he really wanted to ask. "How much does this cost?"

Ms. Rahbull paused, and said in an angelic voice, "Murphy, have you considered what it is worth for you to get rid of this problem?" Murphy thought for a moment. *Was this a trap of some kind?* He was sweating even more than his brow. That always happened when he faced tough decisions.

Murphy answered defensively, "I would have to think about it more."

Ms. Rahbull replied, "That's fine, Murphy. Take as long as you need to consider your options."

Murphy was beside himself. *I need help NOW!* he thought. *I'm in a real pickle.* This person was starting to get under his skin. His inner voice started chattering again about how unfair things were, and how he shouldn't ever be put on the spot to make such a weighty decision in a crisis. The chatter started to crest louder and louder and louder over nanoseconds. Then he heard the next words: "Let me know when you are ready. Have a good day, Murphy." And with that, Ms. Rahbull hung up. And all Murphy heard was a loud BOOM! of silence in his head.

Goodness, what had just happened? Murphy hated having silence in his head. He had too much to accomplish to sit around and think about things. But the silence stayed there, echoing in his mind like a thunderclap. *Options,* he thought. If he had had options, he wouldn't have called her in the first place. Boy, he was getting steamed by the second. He wondered how he had gotten himself into this situation in the first place. She asked what it would be worth to get rid of the problem. Well, if he had options, he'd be on his way to solving his problem, wouldn't he? Then it occurred to him. *What does it matter how much it costs? I still need to figure out how to fix this problem.* Murphy wanted desperately to get rid of this uncomfortable feeling of constant worriment. But he did not even know where to begin negotiations. With that last thought he sent her an email, which said:

Dear Ms. Rahbull,

I appreciate your patience with me while I decided what your help would be worth. Your question was difficult to answer quickly. I imagine I could lose everything I've ever worked for, including the reputation I so worked hard to build, and the trust of my family. In some ways those last two virtues are priceless to me. Since you are more accustomed to working with such situations, would you kindly let me know your fees?

When can we start?

Sincerely, Murphy

In an instant a short reply came from Ms. Rahbull:

Dear Murphy,

It sounds like you are ready to get started. My first service is FREE. Please follow the directions on the LINK I send to you. Mr. Hastie will be following your progress, so we do not miss a beat.

Ms. Rahbull

Murphy thought…*free? I wonder how she can do that? I guess I will find out later.* He was anxious to get to it. He was always more comfortable doing something than talking about it.

CHAPTER NINE
THE SECRET VAULT

"Following the path of the unknown leads to the avenue of greatness."

The next day, Murphy received an email from Mr. Hastie with a link in it. The email only said: "Link to Secret Vault. Press when alone and quiet." Sounded easy. Just a hyperlink on the internet. Murphy closed his office door and told his assistant, Rachel, to hold all of his calls. He wanted absolute concentration so he could focus on whatever tasks might be presented to him. Rachel knew Murphy must have a lot on his mind. It wasn't unusual for him to hold calls for practicing his putting or while in a meeting, or taking time to ideate about the business, but he rarely, if ever, closed his office door. She knew this meant he had something especially serious on his mind.

Meanwhile, Murphy left a voicemail for Mac about how things were progressing, noting he would have liked them to go faster. Nevertheless, in his message he said he would call back after he had completed some preliminary tasks he'd been given.

He ended his message by asking, "How does an advisor stay in business by doing free work?" The skeptic in him couldn't resist. Then he told Mac to take care and that he'd talk to him later. It was time to start work on his new tasks.

He took a few deep breaths before mousing over the email and pressing "Link to Secret Vault." BOOM! Suddenly, the lights went out. He was totally in the dark. He wanted to yell for Rachel, but he couldn't utter a sound. He started to see a dim light across the room. It grew brighter. He felt himself floating towards the light until he was in a room of all white. *Is this how astronauts felt in space with weightlessness?* he wondered. Gradually, filing drawers with labels started to appear. *How odd,* he thought. The drawers were numbered, and on the wall in big letters was the word "TASKS". As he looked back at the drawers, the number one drawer opened slowly just by him looking at it. *That's neat!*

As the first task drawer opened, Murphy could see a man at a desk. Why, it was Mac in Murphy's office! Mac was surrounded by piles and piles of Murphy & Co. financial reports. Curious, Murphy reached out to touch one of the reports. Instantly, a video started for the year the report was generated. It showed all the important things that had occurred that year. Although the video ran at super high speed, Murphy knew just what had happened. Somehow Murphy also knew the financial details Mac was reviewing. Without thinking, Murphy touched the next report, and the next report, and the next one. Each time, the report flew into the drawer with a video showing how the business had operated. Murphy thought, *hey this is interesting and easy!* The videos reminded Murphy of what had occurred in Murphy & Co. over the entire past five years. As the last of the reports vanished from Mac's desk, just as quickly the image of Mac and his desk vanished.

In seconds, the second task drawer opened, and a new video started. This time it was Conor, his CPA sitting in the Accountants' Office working on piles and piles of Murphy & Co. taxes. Wow! Conor had a massive pile of taxes with all kinds of names of businesses he had never heard of in the community, until he noticed his business name. With that attention from Murphy, the report zoomed into the drawer, followed by a second, third and finally a fifth annual tax return. Slowly the drawer closed. Again, this happened in what Murphy thought was seconds. When the returns vanished into the drawer, so did Conor.

This phenomenon went on for all seven drawers. Finally, he could see the drawers were loaded with his interim financials, his annual internal statements, his CPA-prepared financial statements, his CPA tax filings, his service marks and trademarks, an analysis of his recurring customer revenues and forecasts. He had a feeling of satisfaction come over him, like confetti falling all around when you celebrate something big.

BOOM! Murphy was back at his desk in his office staring at the desktop screen. The only difference was that the wall clock read 5:00pm. He heard a knock at his door. It was Rachel saying good night. He returned her courtesy with a smile and said he would see her in the morning.

Whoa! That was something. Was it a dream he had? Did he blackout? Perhaps his stress was getting to him. He checked his pulse and he seemed fine. The day seemed to go so fast. As pleasant as he felt, he wondered, *what just happened to me*? He decided to keep his experience today private. He didn't think others would understand and, frankly, he'd have a tough time explaining. He decided to check his email before he left the office. *That's weird*, he thought. The first link email from Mr. Hastie was gone. But there at the top of his unread emails was another from Ms. Rahbull. It read:

Murphy, thank you for doing such quick work on the tasks. I will contact you within a couple weeks. In the meantime, Mr. Hastie will be in touch tomorrow.

CHAPTER TEN
A VISIT TO DOC

"To understand the problem inside, one must understand the teacher."

Murphy was perplexed. This experience was uncomfortable! It was something he dare tell no one, except perhaps his doctor. With that, Murphy called his doctor's office to set up an appointment. He was in luck! There had been a cancellation and he was put on the schedule first thing the next morning. He was relieved as he told himself, *I'm in an awful way lately. Maybe all this stress and worry is getting to me.*

Doc and Murphy met the next day. Doc asked Murphy, "How are things going? What brings you here to see me?" Doc was also a country club member but not in Murphy's foursome, so Murphy felt very comfortable talking with him. Murphy started the story of the business contracts and goods being stalled overseas and his customer woes. Doc said, "Well, that can be enough to make anyone feel out of sorts. Is there anything specific you can put your finger on that's bothering you?"

Murphy hesitated before he spoke, "Doc, yesterday I went to work and sat at my desk to start a project and the moment I dug into this project, I felt like I was in a daze. In fact, when I looked at the clock, what was 8 hours felt like five minutes. I couldn't recall getting anything done."

Doc looked at Murphy and asked, "Murphy, how are you sleeping?"

Murphy replied, "I guess not too well lately. I have all this on my mind about what I must do to save the business."

Doc asked, "Do you have anyone helping you to sort things out?"

"Well, I…uh," and Murphy stopped himself. He didn't want to talk about Ms. Rahbull, or the Link to the Secret Vault.

Doc sensed Murphy was holding back and said, "Listen, Murphy, we all go through tough times in business. And as owners we know how hard it is to ask for help. We don't want to appear vulnerable. But, perhaps, with a referral from a trusted colleague, you can find someone to help you. Let me check you out here physically first to rule these things out."

With that Doc checked his pulse and temperature, listened to his lungs while he took deep breaths, then listened to his heart, took his blood pressure, looked inside his throat and his ears. He then asked Murphy to lay back while he palpated his liver and stomach and checked his pulse at his ankles—something doctors always do when they need time to figure out what to do next. Doc helped him up and said, "Murphy, physically you check out fine. It seems to me that you may have had temporary, short-term amnesia yesterday at your desk. It can happen with unusually high stress. Our mind is wired to shut down at times when we are extremely fearful and overworked. Your lack of sleep is contributing to your mind in overdrive, so it has not rested properly."

Murphy looked at him in agreement, "Yes, that makes some sense."

Doc continued, "What I am going to prescribe is three melatonin each night, one hour before bed. And that should help you get a good night's rest. Over the next week you should be feeling better. Oh, before I forget, two more things if I might make a couple suggestions, Murphy?"

"Sure," said Murphy. "I'm all ears."

Doc said, "Try and limit your screen time an hour before bed as it can hyper-stimulate your mind."

Murphy replied, "Sure thing, Doc. That should be easy. I can grab a few paperbacks to read before bed. That always helps me to get to sleep. What was the other thing, Doc?"

Doc looked him in the eyes with a wise gaze. Doc was always good at providing comforting advice to people when they needed it most. "Murphy, find someone who can help you who isn't a part of the family. I've seen too much heartache occur between family members in business. Someone who is independent can be objective. Find a trusted advisor and they are worth their weight in gold."

Murphy felt this was a message encouraging him to keep progressing with Ms. Rahbull. "Thanks, Doc. I'll get on it right away and let you know how I make out," Murphy replied as he was leaving Doc's office. Murphy agreed with Doc to pick up a bottle of melatonin at the drugstore on his way home. With that, Doc wished him good luck and Murphy left to return to work, somewhat relieved he wasn't going crazy.

CHAPTER ELEVEN
THE SECOND HASTIE EMAIL

"What we see is never the whole truth."

Heading back to his office, Murphy wondered what was next on his agenda. When he settled into his leather chair behind his desktop computer, there was another email message from Mr. Hastie. *Funny*, he thought, *none of these messages are going to my phone.* That was probably a good thing. If you think texting and driving is bad, pressing a "Link to Secret Vault." while driving could be a catastrophe! He carefully read Mr. Hastie's email.

Dear Murphy,

Attached is a short business self-assessment to complete and return as soon as possible.

Mr. Hastie

Murphy quickly opened the document and read its introduction. *This is interesting*, he thought, as he read the topics and descriptions of business characteristics. There were 50+ factors on which he was supposed to rate his business through the eyes of a buyer. *Why a buyer?* thought Murphy. *I'm not selling the business. I'm trying to stay in business! Looks like I have some homework to do here.* With that, Murphy started to answer each category until he had completed the entire assessment. He was a doer when it came to tasks. He put down what first came to mind in each category. After reviewing it, he attached it to the email and sent it back to Mr. Hastie with a note: "Here ya' go!"

Within seconds, Mr. Hastie wrote back:

Dear Murphy,

Thank you. Attached is a Wish List to outline what you want to accomplish. Please complete it and return to me as soon as possible.

Mr. Hastie

What in the world is a "Wish List?" thought Murphy. Before he opened the document, there were instructions to read. The instructions explained all business owners and businesses are unique and therefore their business wants and needs are unique as well. Depending upon the circumstances facing the owner, the Wish List could include any immediate improvement or any longer-term goal to achieve.

Murphy considered the pickle he was in with his overseas suppliers and his customer contracts. *That's #1 right now!* he thought. Murphy certainly wanted to feel more comfortable about his business being able to survive this calamity. He wrote that down. Soon, he had a flood of thoughts about what he wanted out of the business. He wanted to send his children to college, have the freedom to travel with Mary, and have enough to one day retire from business and live comfortably. He wanted less pressure and to groom someone to take care of the business while he was away from it. He wanted to have some fun at the business and watch it grow and develop. He wanted a little less pressure and risk. On and on and on he wrote, capturing his wants and needs on the Wish List.

When he completed it, he attached the Wish List and sent it to Mr. Hastie once again the same day. His email response was simple: "Here ya' go, again!" Mr. Hastie replied with a note thanking him for his attention to these tasks and that he would be in touch in the next couple of days. That reminded him suddenly that he had not spoken with Liam, his banker, for a few days. Dread suddenly came over him. He decided to check back in with Mac.

CHAPTER TWELVE
UPDATE FOR MAC

"Encouragement lights the wick of dreams."

Murphy dialed up Mac as soon as he finished his work for Mr. Hastie. He was feeling anxious about not talking with Liam and thought it would be good to get some advice before calling.

Mac answered, "Hey, Murphy! How are you doing?"

"Well, it's certainly been interesting," said Murphy. "Seems like I am losing my mind at times. How did you find Ms. Rahbull and Mr. Hastie?"

Mac laughed, "I, too, had a crisis in my business years ago and was referred to Ms. Rahbull. She was so pleasant to work with and before you know it, she had me re-oriented to make the most important decisions in my business."

Murphy went on, "I just had this crazy experience, losing track of time like a dream that drawers were being filled with reports. In fact, you were sitting at my desk going through them!"

"Yes, that sounds just like my first experience with the Secret Vault," said Mac. "You'll be happy to know that Ms. Rahbull is surely working on your valuation as we speak. She doesn't leave much to chance when she's providing advice."

Murphy felt relieved that he wasn't going crazy and was glad Mac had confirmed his experience. Murphy told Mac he had completed some homework for Mr. Hastie as well.

Mac asked, "Was that the Self-Assessment and Wish List from Mr. Hastie?"

Murphy answered, "Yes, it was. He told me to mark down which rating first came to mind. And then asked me what I wanted to see happen in the business and what I wanted from it."

Mac replied, "Murphy, that is spot on with what I did as well. You are on your way to solving your crisis." With that, Mac said he needed to review a few reports before leaving the office and told Murphy he'd be interested in hearing more as Murphy learned more.

Before hanging up, Murphy told Mac he was concerned about Liam, his banker. Mac sighed. He shared with Murphy that it may be best to approach Liam when Murphy knew more facts about the impact of the supply chain delays and when he had a plan in place to address it. Mac said bankers like to know you have solutions and options when facing difficulties. That made sense to Murphy. He would wait to talk with Liam until after he knew more.

CHAPTER THIRTEEN
THE BANKER'S DILEMMA

"Virtue guides us like a lantern in darkness."

Liam was in his office reading the Wall Street Journal and sipping on a cup of hot mint tea. He had been touching base with many of his customers over the last week and all were being affected by supply chain delays to some extent. Some were worse than others, but no one really knew the extent of the impacts and whether it was a temporary problem or a real crisis brewing.

Liam was a seasoned banker familiar with almost everything that could happen in and to businesses during recessions and depressions. He didn't get too worried by initial reports on television. The media tended to report bad news frequently because people found it more interesting. Bad news was also easier to find than good news. False alarms occurred in every business. The last thing he wanted to do was overreact without having hard facts to support an action.

That placed Liam in a dilemma. *Should I make some calls next week or wait to see what happens on a case-by-case basis?* he thought. He always felt he had a good relationship with each of his customers. So good that his top customers, like Murphy, for instance, would most likely call him and let him know if things were getting serious. Liam decided he would wait it out and see what transpires before making any repeat calls. His customers had earned his trust over the years, and they usually responded favorably when he needed facts to report at weekly customer review committee meetings. He had enough to report for the next week or two. So, Liam decided to wait to hear more from customers like Murphy when they knew more. With that, Liam started to write his reports for his next meeting.

CHAPTER FOURTEEN
A LESSON ON VALUE

"Clarity arrives on the journey of acceptance."

Returning to his office, Murphy wondered if Mac's suggestion to wait to speak with Liam was the best decision. How easily things could unravel if Liam found out Murphy was hiding the truth. In this case though, Murphy realized he didn't know exactly what to tell Liam. He had never addressed operational difficulties with his banker. Bankers were all about risk, not operations. Murphy was a realist. That made him naturally skeptical and in the eyes of other owners, a pessimist. Murphy liked Liam and wanted Liam to be his long-term banker. He would have to live with that inner conflict for another week or so until things became clearer.

When he opened his email, Murphy saw there was a message from Mr. Hastie to arrange an appointment with Ms. Rahbull about Value. Murphy responded to set it that afternoon.

He wanted to get some things off his mind. *It would be good to talk with Ms. Rahbull and Mr. Hastie again*, thought Murphy.

To Murphy's surprise, the meeting started with more questions than answers. While Mr. Hastie took copious notes, Ms. Rahbull said that she wanted to make sure her findings were accurate, and that Murphy was the only one who could address her many questions. First, she asked about each topic Murphy crafted on his Owner's Wish List. She wanted to make sure that she had the top priorities for her assignment. Murphy agreed that operating the business with optimism and confidence despite current events would always be high in priority. Murphy then provided input on what he wanted from the business.

He wanted a financial return equal to the many sacrifices he made to run it. Otherwise, he would be an employee of someone else. Then, Murphy admitted he was growing tired of reacting to the event-of-the-day, meaning he wanted to have some consistency and resilience built into his business for rainy days. With that, Ms. Rahbull was satisfied she had Murphy's desires for the business prioritized.

Ms. Rahbull asked about areas on the self-assessment Murphy rated high and low. Ms. Rahbull indicated that these Factors could become areas of potential improvement. She concentrated on areas of Opportunity and Risk. One low-rated factor that stood out was concentration of supplier. Murphy agreed that this one right now was the biggest issue he was facing. Ms. Rahbull went on to cover all the factors so she could confirm and prioritize her recommendations.

As Ms. Rahbull's Value Lesson began, Murphy asked, "Ms.

Rahbull, what does your valuation tell you about my business? How much is it worth?"

Ms. Rahbull replied, "We are calculating a preliminary Value which isn't very helpful until we have all the pieces of the puzzle. Attributes like recurring revenue, concentration of customer, business attractiveness, and other characteristics of the business add or detract from Value. More importantly, we need to make sure we have captured those from our discussions."

Mr. Hastie could be heard typing away on his keyboard. Murphy figured he would get a quick answer to stop the questions rolling around in his head. But Ms. Rahbull was firm, "Murphy, when you look back on this exercise, do you want something you can rely upon to build value?"

Murphy immediately responded, "Yes, precisely!"

Ms. Rahbull agreed. "Now let's talk about Value." Murphy was all ears.

Murphy listened intently as Ms. Rahbull explained how a business value was reached. She outlined that the conclusion, Fair Market Value (FMV), is in its simplest sense the price an asset would sell for on the open market. Murphy understood that—his goods were valued by customers based on supply and demand in any given year. This year, artificial Christmas trees were in high demand and customers were willing to pay a premium if they found one. Ms. Rahbull continued, "FMV represents the price of an asset under the following usual set of conditions: prospective buyers and sellers are reasonably knowledgeable about the asset, behaving in their own best interest, free of undue pressure to trade, and given a reasonable time for completing the transaction."

Murphy immediately understood the concept. He had never

thought about his business in those terms because he thought valuations were only for business owners who were selling their business. He asked, "Ms. Rahbull, isn't a valuation only needed if you are interested in selling your business?"

Ms. Rahbull replied, "Only if you want to be surprised at the most critical time when you need to know. Our valuation is performed for planning and preparation purposes. So when the time comes for you to sell or transfer the business, you have no surprises."

Murphy paused in thought. He liked no surprises in business because it agreed with his business philosophy. It was getting frustrating by having to react day in and day out.

Ms. Rahbull then asked Murphy if she could elaborate to make this easy for him to better understand. Ms. Rahbull asked Murphy if his CPA had provided him the business' Earnings Before Interest Taxes, Depreciation, and Amortization (EBITDA) for last year. Murphy expressed that Conor hadn't provided anything like that. Ms. Rahbull went on, "Let's say your EBITDA is $500,000 a year. We take that EBITDA and by evaluating your business factors we arrive at a Multiple. For instance, if your Multiple is 4, as the business stands today, we take 4 times the EBITDA to calculate Fair Market Value. In that example your business value is $2,000,000. Does that make sense?"

Murphy thought for a minute. He asked, "If it's that easy, why are you in business?"

Ms. Rahbull smiled. "Murphy, the multiplication is easy. The Multiple is the challenge and the art of valuation! The work starts with an initial valuation. That's merely a photo at a point in time of your business. The real goal is to help you achieve a higher Multiple and to grow your EBITDA at the same time to measure against another point in time down the road. Two photos you can compare."

Murphy exclaimed, "I get it!" He thought of Mac's recent weight loss preparing for surgery. "It's like comparing the before and after pictures when losing weight!"

"Well, not exactly, Murphy. But seeing the difference is encouraging in both situations." said Ms. Rahbull.

"What do we do now?" asked Murphy.

Ms. Rahbull said, "Murphy, we move forward and calculate a Fair Market Value for your business for the purpose of planning and preparation. Then we orient to what goals you have and determine if there are any gaps in what you want and what the business can deliver today. It may be that you will want to make some changes over a short time to improve and adapt the business to meet those goals. At that point, Murphy, you will have built-in Value protection. And we can eventually talk about what new options are available to you. Does that sound like a reasonable approach?"

Murphy felt a bit of relief knowing there was a path to determine value, but he still didn't have a solution to get his goods delivered if the world shut down trade. He figured he would check back in with Mac to see if his cousin had some insight from his own experiences. In the meantime, he agreed with Ms. Rahbull, "Looks like a good plan," and after saying goodbye to her and Mr. Hastie, a glimmer of hope was extinguished by his next thought...*as long as I can stay in business.*

CHAPTER FIFTEEN
A LESSON ON READINESS

*"Mysteries in life are revealed in small steps. Miracles occur
more often than we realize."*

Murphy called Mac to check in with him on his Value lesson.
He told Mac about the valuation process and how meticulous
Ms. Rahbull was with her explanation and the simplicity of
it all.

Mac chuckled, "Murphy, some of the most obvious things in
life aren't so obvious."

"How's that?" asked Murphy.

Mac went on, "It seems that most business owners are
willing to work hard to obtain a goose that lays golden eggs, but
they don't understand they need to take care of the goose and
protect the golden eggs laid over the years." Murphy had never
considered his business as a goose. Mac continued, "Some
owners find that every time the goose lays a golden egg, they go
out and borrow against it. That's when a lifestyle owner can get

into financial trouble, being highly leveraged by payments and debt. The goose turns into a golden noose."

Murphy laughed out loud. "Mac, you really have a way with words! But I understand what you are saying. If you spend as much as you make and something goes haywire in your business, how will you be able to respond?"

"That's exactly the point, Murphy!" Continuing his line of thought, Mac said, "Think of it this way: what would it be like for you to have the business ready for anything that comes your way? Something you could use to support making those critical or creative decisions, because you have a Value Test?" Murphy listened intently.

Then Mac made a bottom-line statement that hit home with Murphy. "Here's the reason for preparing your business and knowing your Value, Murphy. At any time, for any reason, the business can be transferred for maximum value, regardless of choice or chance events. In other words, why would you not take care of and protect the goose that has 85% of your wealth tied up in it? Why wouldn't you be ready for opportunity to knock and at the same time be ready for a calamity to strike?"

Murphy replied with a question, "I guess you could be lazy, a non-believer in Value, or maybe not understand the Value of the goose. Or if, like you said, something bad happens by chance, then being ready helps to protect the goose?"

"Precisely!" said Mac. "It's like winning both ways when you start understanding how Value works and how it is built. Protecting the goose is like being self-insured for your financial future."

Mac sat back in his chair while Murphy absorbed the Readiness lesson. Murphy contemplated the potential impacts, negative ones first, of course, since he was a pessimist. Now, he was seeing a different side of his pessimism. Perhaps with this Value and Readiness lesson, he could make better decisions in business and react less. That would be inspiring instead of tiring. He counted on his goose to lay golden eggs and take care of him and his family. Taking care of the goose was important. Mac had driven home his lesson to Murphy. But he wasn't finished.

CHAPTER SIXTEEN

A LESSON ON TIMING

"Rely on intuition and follow your heart in all things."

Murphy thought Mac's lessons were over until Mac started to bring up one more topic: Timing. Murphy had heard about this from his buddies at the country club many, many times over. The conversation always started out that so-and-so did such-and-such and boy, was his timing good in getting out when he did. It was always timing! Of course, no one ever talked about the unlucky ones who didn't get out. Those stories were like curses to repeat. How could someone become a slave to their business because of debt and liabilities? Those owners were looked down upon as downright DUMB! But in the back of every owner's mind there's a voice of truth that echoes loudly from experience. It produces an admixture of dread with a friendly warning message: *One day it could happen to you*! Owners don't like hearing that voice. Murphy's country club buddies never spoke about the unlucky ones, even though they knew they existed.

Mac proceeded to outline his view on timing as Murphy returned from his thoughts. "Murphy, all the guys at the country club talk about timing this, timing that, when someone succeeds. You'd think someone had cornered the market on timing. And that's just not the truth. You can't time the markets. You can't time chance events. And you can't time the goose's laying golden eggs. It doesn't happen that way."

Murphy asked, "So how does timing occur in your favor?"

Mac proceeded, "You make timing irrelevant."

BOOM! Murphy couldn't believe what Mac had just said. "What do you mean, Mac? How do you make timing irrelevant? Isn't it all about timing?"

Mac leaned in, "Murphy, once the business has peak attractiveness to any potential buyer and you've value-prepped it to be ready for anything it faces—by chance or by choice—you have made timing irrelevant."

Murphy was skeptical, as he always heard stories at the country club to the contrary. "Can you tell me more?" asked Murphy.

Mac began by telling Murphy that the way to make timing irrelevant was this rule: "Know Thy Value." According to Mac, once you understand your Value you can protect your goose and its golden eggs. Minimally, you mitigate risks and maximize returns given any circumstances, so it does not kill the goose. Mac went on to talk about finding the drivers of Value – actions that enhance Value so that, if you concentrate on them, Value rises. Mac also explained that there were detractors of Value— actions that you need to take in order to reduce waste and excess. Mac seemed to understand much more about Value than he ever led on. *Gosh*, Murphy thought, *if I had only known, I would have paid more attention to Value before this crisis occurred.* He hoped that it wasn't too late to positively affect his future.

CHAPTER SEVENTEEN

PROGRESS MADE

"In times of scarcity, anything will satisfy.
In times of prosperity, nothing may satisfy."

While Murphy was finishing up at the office the next day, news arrived from overseas that looked like a small flicker of light at the end of the tunnel. The email from his major supplier indicated it could shift many products Murphy & Co. had ordered from ocean containers to air freight. These same air carriers were being used to bring supplies for the pandemic to assist the country of origin, and in their return flights to the United States, they were backhauling general freight to offset costs.

Murphy picked up the phone, called Michael, his Logistics Manager, and discussed what air freight may mean to his costs. Michael was already talking to James, the Sales Manager, and Patricia, the Customer Care Manager, to understand which contracts they had in place where freight would be absorbed by customers. It turned out that 80% of the customers were paying for freight. Before making any arrangements, James was having his salesforce call all the customers to see if they could and would accept air freight charges. The whole supply chain was being affected. To Murphy, air freight looked expensive, nevertheless it was an option he hadn't had two weeks ago. And for that he was grateful. It looked like some progress was being made on the overseas front and everyone was working hard to find solutions for their customers.

Murphy noticed a buzz on his phone. Mr. Hastie was in his voicemail. Before leaving, he listened to his message. Tomorrow, Mr. Hastie and Ms. Rahbull had time to review the final valuation for Murphy's business. They knew Murphy wanted to move things forward as fast as possible. Armed with Mac's lessons on business value, readiness, and timing, Murphy decided it was an important meeting to set. With the new revelations on logistics in the works, Murphy felt confident that knowing more about his goose was better before the crisis turned into a catastrophe. He emailed Mr. Hastie promptly that 9:00am would be best for him. As he drove home from the distribution center that evening, he couldn't think of a better way to end his day. *Other than an Irish coffee after dinner*, he thought.

CHAPTER EIGHTEEN

A VALUABLE PRESENTATION

"Expectations can be the path to achievement or disappointment.
Therefore, make certain you understand what it is you want."

Murphy arrived at the office at 7:00am, before the office officially opened, a habit formed early in his career. It was a quiet chunk of time when he could prepare for meetings or review reports and key performance indicators without interruptions. Key measures were reviewed on his Executive Dashboard report, like percentage of accurate deliveries on-time and shipments loaded out in less than 4 hours.

He felt more relaxed than normal, although he didn't have all the answers. He thought maybe it was because he was learning something new that could have significant meaning to his routine. That brought a bit of excitement to the forefront of his normally pessimistic outlook. Then again, he hadn't heard answers to his questions of Value of his business. He was worried what the report may reveal. With butterflies in his stomach, he prepared himself to hear any bad news.

Ms. Rahbull and Mr. Hastie arrived 5 minutes early and were greeted by Rachel who offered them something to drink and escorted them to the Conference Room where they could review their presentation with Murphy confidentially. The presentation started when Murphy arrived. After a warm and friendly hello, Ms. Rahbull opened the meeting by handing a presentation to Murphy with the title: Murphy & Co.'s Value-Prep Plan. It was bound in a three-ring binder. There was also a PowerPoint presentation on the laptop being projected for Murphy to watch. Murphy thought that was very professionally prepared.

The Value-Prep Plan presentation included information on his business, spreadsheets of his annual profit and loss and balance sheets over five years, projections into the next five years and value points to be made in several areas of the business. The presentation addressed financial comparisons and ratios, backed with data that Murphy had seen go into the Secret Vault. It was a thorough and accurate representation of his business' financial history and showed the results of Average EBITDA and Weighted EBITDA, which Murphy now paid close attention to as a measure.

Overall, Murphy was following along with ease. His talks with Mac helped pave the way to ask intelligent questions about the valuation process. The value range was then revealed. Murphy had wondered how his business would be valued and there it was in print. They even showed him what value was after-taxes that could be invested. He nodded his head as Ms. Rahbull wrapped up her value conclusions. She asked, "Murphy, is this value what you expected?"

Murphy sat back in his chair and said, "It's lower than I

expected, but it looks fair and reasonable based on the data you shared. The point of the process is to use this for planning and preparation, correct?"

Ms. Rahbull replied, "Yes, Murphy. This report is for internal planning purposes and provides a Fair Market Value range for what we are seeing in the marketplace today. It is a starting point for us to continue the conversation after you've thought more about what you want from the business. We do have a separate recommendation for you."

Murphy looked interested. Mr. Hastie asked, "Do you have a Personal Financial Plan that tells you how much you will need for your children's college education and for your retirement?" He added, "Have you done any planning for what you may need after-tax to support your lifestyle in retirement?" Murphy thought for a minute and said he had considered using someone to help him figure that out but being so busy it never became a priority. Frankly, one of the biggest hurdles was not knowing how much his business was worth.

Mr. Hastie indicated he had a couple of advisors Murphy could interview who were Certified Financial Planners, the kind of people who would help Murphy build out his personal wealth plan. Murphy asked, "Why is that important to business value?"

Mr. Hastie had a coaching moment with Murphy. "The majority of a privately-held business owner's wealth is built around extracting that Value in a sale or a transfer. Your Personal Financial Plan is built around the Value you have in your business, along with other assets like your home and liquid investments like ETF's, mutual funds, stocks, and bonds. Since most owners have 70%-85% of their wealth invested in their businesses, that's a pretty big number. That also means you need a business Value you can count on when you have so much at risk."

Murphy considered Mr. Hastie's suggestion and he decided it was time to start working with a Certified Financial Planner to get the bigger picture of how business Value affects him and his family. With that, the meeting ended. Ms. Rahbull suggested that Murphy think about his valuation. She said the next step would include doing a Value Gap Analysis, the difference between the amount Murphy wanted after-tax and what amount he would need to close that gap in business Value by adapting to a Value Mindset. Murphy was starting to feel some momentum build as the pieces of the puzzle were coming together. Everyone shook hands and agreed to meet soon to further evaluate what needed to be changed in the business. In the meantime, Murphy would meet with one of the trusted referrals from Mr. Hastie and learn more about what he needed and wanted out of the business.

CHAPTER NINETEEN
THE PERSONAL FINANCIAL PLAN

"Do not mistake inner peace for contentment. Once you know inner peace, you may no longer be content."

Murphy looked at his phone. There was a text from Mac. It said, "Hey Murphy! Forgot to mention the other day that you might want to take the time to review your personal goose." Murphy smiled. Mac was clairvoyant at times. It was almost as if he had been in the presentation meeting with Mr. Hastie. Arriving at the office at his normal 7:00am, he went to his office and noticed an inner feeling of calm. That was unusual. He was always running hither and thither in a frizz-frazz at work. But not today.

He found in his emails an introduction from Mr. Hastie to two personal financial planners. He Googled both names and saw that each was credentialed and had credible experience and backgrounds. He placed a call to each advisor and was fortunate to be able to talk directly to them as they were early risers too, which he liked. He discussed what he was looking for and how he had been working closely with Ms. Rahbull and Mr. Hastie. Murphy asked if they would prefer a Zoom or an in-person call to gather some details. Both indicated either would work and that it would be about an hour investment of time for an introductory meeting. Because this was a preliminary meeting, and Murphy was concerned about leaving the business amid a crisis, he opted for a Zoom call with each advisor.

Just as Mr. Hastie relayed to him, both were eager to help, and both were very knowledgeable. Murphy explained his current project with business preparation and the recent Value presentation, and said he was looking to evaluate his personal financial situation. He told both advisors he would speak with his wife, Mary, before making any decision. One advisor, Catherine, suggested that his wife be at the next meeting. That was the tie breaker! Murphy made the decision to meet with Catherine the next day.

Murphy and Mary met with Catherine and felt very comfortable speaking with her. She asked about their family assets, if they used an annual expense budget, their income sources, the ages of their four children, desire for post-secondary opportunities for education at university or vocational colleges, and on and on and on. Her list of questions was almost as long as Mr. Hastie's self-assessment Murphy had completed for the business! Catherine even asked about their dreams and goals. That was the most fun. Catherine indicated she would have a family budget prepared. In addition, she would evaluate their assets and have a draft Personal Financial Plan ready within a week. They could then meet again and discuss her findings.

In the meantime, Mary had a few items she needed to understand so she asked some direct questions and was satisfied with the answers she received. Murphy was pleased at how well Mary and Catherine interacted. He could tell Catherine had the experience and the background to do this kind of planning. He was glad he had invited Mary on this adventure. Overall, it was an easy process. When Murphy returned to the office, he felt even more relieved that things were coming together. Now he thought, if only the business crisis would subside, he'd be in really good spirits.

CHAPTER TWENTY

PROBLEM, CRISIS, OR CATASTROPHE?

"Resourcefulness finds options when seemingly none exist."

While the Certified Financial Planner was working on Murphy and Mary's Financial Plan, Ms. Rahbull was compiling a short list of financial items that would be good discussion points on Murphy's Balance Sheet and Income Statement. Meanwhile, Murphy continued to stay on top of his business crisis and the potential for goods arriving on-time from overseas. The team at Murphy & Co. had been contacting customers and, for the most part, every customer wanted to air freight the goods in, if necessary. Things were also starting to look brighter as world news was reporting this pandemic virus was unexpectedly short-lived. Murphy understood the health reports were early. Until he knew for certain that his manufacturer was back at work and shipping goods, he was admittedly feeling pessimistic.

That afternoon, Murphy, Michael, James, and Patricia met to share updates on Customer Care, Sales, and Logistics. They concluded that it was still possible to obtain goods if the crisis turned around overseas in the next two weeks. That window, once closed, would necessitate air freighting the finished goods to Murphy & Co or directly to customer's docks. In the meantime, they were preparing a contingency plan to execute for the air freight and logistics requirements. Murphy listened intently. He was proud of his team and trusted their judgment. Michael, the Team Leader, indicated he had direct contact with the plant overseas and he was being given updates every day, including weekends. That meant workers in the offices had not left, only production folks.

Since it was late in the production year for all overseas manufacturers, most finished goods were in containers in their yards or in their massive warehouses awaiting pick-pack and shipping instructions. At least Murphy knew from experience that the goods were available. With that the meeting concluded, and everyone was assigned a new task for the next weekly meeting update. After that meeting, Murphy left the Conference Room and returned to his office. Surprisingly, his email had only one message from overseas and it confirmed what he had heard from his Crisis Team.

His mobile phone rang, and it was Mr. Hastie. Mr. Hastie wanted to know if Murphy and Mary had selected a Certified Financial Planner. Murphy acknowledged that they had indeed selected one of the two referrals, and that Catherine was working on their Personal Financial Plan. Mr. Hastie asked when Murphy thought he'd be receiving their Personal Financial Plan. Murphy relayed Catherine's promise to provide it by the end of the week. Mr. Hastie was delighted to hear that news. Ms. Rahbull wanted to set the next meeting to discuss what Murphy and his wife Mary would need from the business, after-tax, to continue to enjoy their lifestyle for many years. Murphy agreed to first thing next Tuesday in the evening at the office around 6:00pm. Mary would attend and the four of them would review both plans.

After the call, Murphy began reviewing the business reports and saw that his seasonal draw on his line of credit was normal but remained at mid-high six figures. It reminded him of the devastating consequences of not receiving goods. *Although,* he thought, *we are doing everything we can within our control to ensure we are prepared. And this may not turn out to be a crisis after all. It may be one more problem which I've avoided letting escalate into a catastrophe. If that happens, I'll be lucky.* At that moment he made a vow to himself. He'd never be unprepared again in business.

CHAPTER TWENTY-ONE
THE VALUE GAP

"Being persistent is the apprenticeship for mastery."

Tuesday evening came fast as the weekend was filled with family activities for the Murphy clan. Each of the children were involved in something with athletics. Sunday was busy attending Church and making sure everyone was prepared for Monday with their homework assignments completed. Usually on Sundays, they had family dinner together as well. Murphy loved his family and his family life. He looked around the table and realized how important the health of the business was for their future. He had not thought about his ability to provide for them before this latest crisis. Now it seemed so personal. Tomorrow he and Mary would get the Personal Financial Plan and on Tuesday they would talk with Ms. Rahbull and Mr. Hastie.

On Monday, Murphy and Mary had a Zoom conference call

with Catherine, their new Financial Advisor, who shared the results of the Personal Financial Plan. Murphy and Mary reviewed their budget and saw their needs, wants, and dreams in financial terms. It was eye-opening to see the costs for education, travel, discretionary spending, and the many assumptions they were making like income growth and inflation indexes. Mary and Murphy both agreed on the accuracy of the numbers and the forecast. Murphy focused on one REALLY BIG assumption that indicated how much he would need to accumulate in his business over time. Now he understood why Ms. Rahbull and Mr. Hastie wanted to meet the next day. He noted there was a significant difference between the number he needed on the Personal Financial Plan, and the current after-tax Value he had in the business.

The next evening, Murphy and Mary, Ms. Rahbull, and Mr. Hastie reviewed the numbers from Catherine. It was time to discuss the difference between the current business Value and how much more was needed to close the gap in future Value. Mr. Hastie took the lead on this conversation and Murphy again listened intently, taking notes. Mr. Hastie talked through several scenarios of normal business growth which closed the gap by 50%. Then he asked Murphy to consider where he planned on finding hidden value in his business. Murphy was confused by that question and asked Mr. Hastie to clarify and elaborate on the term "hidden value."

Mr. Hastie likened "hidden value" to those things you take for granted in the business and rarely look at when you don't have a plan. With a plan, they become discovered Opportunities for saving money, time, or both in the business. "If someone has time as an ally," Mr. Hastie commented, "in a short period there may be operational savings that yield the other 50% easily. For instance, if you save $100,000 and you are able to enhance your Multiple from 4X to 5X by working on your Operating Costs to increase EBITDA, you have a $500,000 improvement in Value."

Ah! Murphy instantly remembered the power of the Multiple. "What you are saying, Mr. Hastie, is that I don't have to find the whole 50%, correct?" asked Murphy. "I only need to find 10% savings to yield me the 50% on a 5X Multiple." Mr. Hastie beamed with pride as he knew Murphy now understood the leverage in a Multiple. Immediately, Murphy started calculating in his head what normal organic growth would provide him and what options he had for saving costs and growing income strategically. The possibilities started to get clearer.

Ms. Rahbull then made an interesting observation. "Murphy, if you would create a cross-functional team, like you have done now in a crisis, that Value Team could be working for you on the business and provide ways to close your Value Gap more quickly. With the years ahead of you, I would say that it's possible you could be getting more value appreciation with Murphy & Co. than is conservatively portrayed in your Personal Financial Plan."

Murphy sat back in his conference room chair and thought for a moment. Could this be true? He would need to sleep on it and most likely he would have questions tomorrow. If Ms. Rahbull and Mr. Hastie were right, he could be on track for some wonderful years ahead. Murphy responded, "Ms. Rahbull, I can see that potential now. I never knew what I needed from the business, and this makes it perfectly clear. I suppose Value is the one thing I must pay attention to more than anything else."

Ms. Rahbull smiled at Mary and said, "Your Murphy is a

good student." Mary smiled and knew her husband had worked hard and smart over the years. Now she more fully appreciated what those qualities meant to them as a family. Murphy finally smiled, which made Mary even happier.

CHAPTER TWENTY-TWO

PROBLEM SOLVED, CRISIS AVOIDED

"Joy and peace arrive when gratitude thrives."

Two days later, an email arrived indicating the plant overseas was reopening in a week. The crisis was avoided thanks to Mother Nature creating a strain of virus that didn't last very long. It died out shortly after it spread. Murphy & Co. was now back in business, readying for the containers of seasonal goods from their overseas manufacturer. Miraculously, they would be on-time.

Murphy looked back on the last 4 weeks, considering all he had learned. He was grateful, very grateful. For the support he had from his wife and family, who understood he was in a crisis. For Mac, who was a sounding board and understood what Murphy was confronting. For the referral he received to Ms. Rahbull and Mr. Hastie, and then their referral to Catherine, the Certified Financial Planner. Murphy was indebted with gratitude for everyone who had helped him. His Crisis Team of

Michael, James and Patricia dove into the overseas problem and worked collaboratively to layout a contingency plan. He was proud of their performance under such stress. Murphy felt a wave of gratefulness blanket him. He couldn't believe how he had learned the positive effects of the single most important decision to Value-Prep the business. In doing so, Murphy had one more question to clarify with Ms. Rahbull. How did Value-Prep protection work?

CHAPTER TWENTY-THREE
VALUE PROTECTION

"No one gets everything they want. Everyone usually can get most of what they want."

Murphy placed a call to Ms. Rahbull after sleeping on that one question from their meeting the night before. He really wanted to understand value protection. In fact, Murphy wrote it down at 3:00am on his notepad by the bed to remind himself. Ms. Rahbull answered her phone immediately, "Hi, Murphy! How are you?"

Murphy replied, "Probably better than I've been in a bunch of months, Ms. Rahbull." Murphy sounded full of vim and vigor.

Ms. Rahbull could hear Murphy's energy over the phone. Ms. Rahbull asked, "What can I do for you, Murphy?" She was so pleasant and easy to talk with about almost anything.

Murphy jumped right in, "I want to understand how Value-Prepping creates a 'self-insured' protection."

Ms. Rahbull replied, "In simplest terms, Murphy, events in life happen by choice or by chance. When sudden, chance events occur and the owner's business is not prepared, it turns a crisis into a catastrophe. No one really knows what to do. The business is at the mercy of fate. The family income may be jeopardized seriously. Remember, many owners have everything in their head. They don't leave instructions for anyone. Systems may not be in place to handle routine processes for business continuance. And the business may slip from a going concern to a business in distress."

"Well, I have a management team," said Murphy. "Isn't that enough?"

"Not really, Murphy," said Ms. Rahbull. "It is a key piece of the plan, but protection needs to come in a few forms. For instance, any sudden event like death, disability, divorce, distress, or disagreement among stakeholders can place the business at risk. Having a management team helps. But if they fight over who is leader, then there's distress and disagreement. A business that has been prepared properly can withstand those chance events, and that's the element of protection that Value-Prep provides. There are very few surprises that become a catastrophe as the organization continues to pursue Value."

Murphy asked, "So what else can I do to protect the business?"

Ms. Rahbull answered, "Staying organized with written processes and systems is a start. Having a Letter of Guidance stored by your Executive Assistant in a safe place can leave instructions for others in an emergency."

Murphy responded, "I never thought of that, Ms. Rahbull. If something happened to me for even three months in a rehab hospital, what would my management team do? There does need to be a leader in place on-site and the Letter of Guidance sounds like instructions that would help."

"These things need to be carefully thought out, Murphy." said Ms. Rahbull. "When you are prepared and organized to handle the worst scenario, it usually never happens." That made sense to Murphy.

CHAPTER TWENTY-FOUR
ADVISORS FOR LIFE

"Good fortune has much to do with deliberate practice."

Before he left the call, he had one final question for Ms. Rahbull which he'd been thinking about for some time "What do I pay you for doing all this work?

Ms. Rahbull said, "Murphy, if you want us to work with you quarterly to help monitor your progress, we can provide you a proposal on using Simplified Value-Prep®. If you want access to Mr. Hastie or me, for phone calls and guidance in between that time, we can include that as well. Would you like it proposed monthly, quarterly, or annually?" Murphy thought for a moment and said, "That depends."

Ms. Rahbull continued, "I'd recommend you keep the Simplified Value-Prep® confidential vault in place. It's a small monthly subscription that can be paid annually for a discount. The vault can hold a Letter of Guidance with a security classification only you and one other person have available. In addition, you may want us to talk with some of your key managers and do a mini presentation on Value, if you want to use Value in your business to direct their thinking and management behaviors. There are a few ways we could assist you as you grow your business Value. Now that you have done the Value-Prep work, you understand how powerful it can be. We would enjoy working with you to reach your business financial goals." Murphy asked Ms. Rahbull to send a proposal to him and he would review it. Murphy said good-bye and called Mac.

"Hey, Mac," said Murphy, "I just want to thank you again for the referral to Ms. Rahbull and Mr. Hastie. I think we are going to engage them as Value Advisors to the business. I've been thinking about creating an Advisory Board to help me on the next steps in expansion of the company. Ms. Rahbull or Mr. Hastie could be very helpful. What do you think?"

Mac replied, "Murphy, you've come a long way in a short period of time with their help. I imagine that would be a good investment, especially if you expect to grow. And the Advisory Board is something I've heard works well for many owners."

Murphy paused and said, "Mac, you wouldn't believe how valuable their advice has been to me. With the referral to the Certified Financial Planner, we've been able to put together our family wealth building plan. It may take some years, but we now have goals and a solid plan moving forward to help us. I am excited about my business again and even more so about our family's financial future. It took a ton of weight off my shoulders knowing we are working on things financially for the long-term, while we enjoy our time together. And all it took was a business crisis and Value-Prep to get me on the right track!"

Mac was smiling on the other end of the phone hearing how Murphy had come a long way from his pessimistic outlook. The change was remarkable. Mac could not resist asking Murphy, "I guess you are finally a believer in being prepared?"

Murphy replied, "I'd recommend it to every business owner."

Mac chuckled with satisfaction. He knew Murphy had learned the most influential lesson in business about value, and that would change his business outlook forever. Mac then asked the million-dollar question, "So, Murphy, what is your philosophy about business now?"

Murphy, a little sheepishly responded, gradually growing louder as he said, "If something can go wrong, it usually will... UNLESS YOU ARE PREPARED!" They both broke into the belly laughs characteristic of their close family relationship and said good-bye to one another.

EPILOGUE: MURPHY & CO

"Passion fuels action towards our potential."

Two years later, Murphy & Co. with the help of their advisors, grew 30% per year in revenues and 40% in Net Income. Their EBITDA grew substantially, and consequently so did their Value. Everyone in the company enjoyed a Value orientation and bonus. It was refreshing knowing each employee had their minds, hands, and hearts in their work. It was an attractive place to work. The community was enhanced through their increased donations. Liam the Banker was as happy as ever that Murphy & Co. was his client. People were happy at work.

Murphy had outgrown his warehouse and was considering a new facility for expansion. He also had his eye on a Mid-West acquisition. Murphy had become a keen strategist over the past two years. His newly created position of CFO was someone he trusted and had promoted from within. Murphy continued to support continuing education in every department. The company had the reputation of being family-oriented and "a best place to work" for the last two years.

On the personal financial side, Murphy and Mary were banking monies earmarked for educations for their four children. They took a couple vacations a year with the children and a couple without the children. Murphy had entrusted his Management Team to operate the business with the authority they needed to fulfill their responsibilities to one another. Murphy couldn't have been happier.

Life was good because his business was good. Just as Murphy had prepared it to be.

AUTHOR'S NOTES

"Being adaptable means working through and around
challenges in business. It is a survivor's trait."

THEORY OF READINESS™ & SIMPLIFIED VALUE-PREP®

I am a former deal junkie. As an M&A Advisor for 16 years I was focused on the lower middle market selling clients' businesses. Our firm served privately held businesses with values from $2 Million to $50 Million. We operated under full contingency, meaning we were paid only if we were successful. This was a huge risk, as any given transaction represented 800-1200 hours of work by our team. As you will see, my early career lessons as a former business owner and then financial turnaround executive congealed in performing M&A advisory work with other business owners.

I had the benefit as a turnaround executive of leading businesses in deep financial trouble caused by poor owner choices, neglect of fundamentals of financial accountability and inconsistent management. The businesses were mired in poor leadership, fragmented direction, flavor-of-the-day decisions coupled with negative, chance events that occurred beyond anyone's control. You might call it the perfect storm for a business catastrophe! I was able to lead these organizations through difficulty by identifying root causes and re-orienting them to flourish. I assimilated my ownership experiences and implemented those lessons to change the business' trajectory. Oftentimes, I wondered how these businesses and their owners had been lucky to overcome the insurmountable odds of survival. Had they continued the same behaviors before I arrived, the businesses certainly would have been liquidated. In each case, I noted what steps I had taken and the key changes that occurred internally and externally. Most importantly, I recognized how each of those businesses was turned around financially to eventually become valuable assets for the family business owners to sell.

In my subsequent family office work, the financial stakes rose even higher for my clients. They were faced with multiple devastating events over five years. The first was the Great Recession of 2007-2009. That one event placed the entire portfolio of operating assets in jeopardy of liquidation. To add to that financial crisis, the mental disability of a co-founder created a chain of other events that impacted the business partnerships. Disagreement reigned between general partners, family members became estranged, critical franchise licenses were terminated, the divorce of a co-founder and death of a co-founder became more fuel for the financial fire. So, when you think you have trouble in your business, there is some perspective for you to consider. Several of these challenges even occurred at the same time!

Through sheer perseverance and reliance on my acquired business instincts, I applied what I had learned as a business owner and in-house turnaround executive. Collaborating with the co-owners' long-time CPAs and legal counsel, we navigated through these treacherous chance events. Managing crises with strategic planning and preparation, the family's business assets doubled in five years. The owners decided it was time to de-risk and execute an exit, which I was prepared to lead. It was a remarkable success, and a chapter of my career I would never forget.

My curiosity was still at work. Diving deeper into how this transformation had occurred gave me pause to reflect. As I replayed the big picture options we created and the co-owners' right decisions, I questioned if there was more to this successful value transformation than met the eye. That was the moment in which elements of the preparation process began to take shape.

As an M&A Advisor, I enjoyed learning the unique Value Drivers in each business, and it was especially satisfying taking a company to market when it was prepared. As a deal under-writer, I was responsible for financial analysis, valuation, testing market comparables, writing the offering memorandum, pack-aging the company for market, and doing pre-market due dili-gence. After the letter-of-intent was signed, I would collaborate with the owner, key management team members, transaction attorneys, and accounting and tax professionals from both buyer and seller, as I shepherded the company through complex due diligence.

These experiences gave me a broad and deep perspective on what both parties wished to achieve, favorable and unfavorable deal points, justification for pricing and terms, the buildup of value, value gap analysis, owner outcome desires, and buyer insights. I collected key business readiness factors that maximized perceived Value. In all cases, maximizing price was based on the transferability of Business Value to the buyer for expected growth. At the same time, I observed that the odds of a successful closing were not in the favor of the seller, unless they had invested time in preparation. Ben Franklin's timeless wisdom *"an ounce of prevention is worth a pound of cure"* echoed true. Nine out of ten businesses were not ready for prime-time sale.

What I found as an M&A advisor was that half of those unprepared businesses would never sell or transfer. These were lifestyle businesses whose owners either started it up or bought a business to have a better-than-average income with the freedom to call the shots, rather than remain an employee. Not surprisingly, lifestyle businesses were not value-building enterprises. Lifestyle owners would drain business cash flow to meet personal wants and needs. When it came time to sell, the lifestyle owner wondered why their personal cash cow did not justify a healthy multiple on a sale. Quite the opposite was true. These lifestyle businesses had everything in the heads of the owners and were not transferrable. Lack of systems and repeatable processes, high concentration of customers, low working capital, risk of owner absence, and other factors made the business unattractive to invest in as a buyer. These businesses were often classified as "turn downs" for sell-side representation due to the likelihood that we would invest hundreds of hours on contingency with no reward for doing so.

For the remaining half of those unprepared business cases, we openly discussed their business' "readiness" to go to market and the option to Value-Prep before doing so. Unfortunately, their decision came at a time when they were already stressed by the thought of letting go and transitioning in their personal lives. Regardless of being cautioned to stay rooted in the present, once many owners mentally made their decision to sell, they were already focusing on how to spend their once-in-a-life-time payday. It was much more enjoyable than being educated in the process and benefits of Value-Prepping. Conflicting priorities such as this were sure signs of trouble ahead, especially during the emotional rollercoaster of negotiations and the sale process. And so we found only one or two owners had the discipline to be patient and work on the business to prepare it, once they had committed in their mind to sell. It was clear to me that Value-Prepping needed to occur as early in the life of the business as was practical, and BEFORE considering a sale of the business. This became the basis for applying Simplified Value-Prep® as a tool for any owner to build and protect business wealth.

Our approach to preparing a business for sale before a sale emanated from the collective wisdom among our team of seasoned advisors that included former business owners, corporate CEOs, and bankers. What became clear to me was that there was no actionable process available to repeat and follow by the unprepared businesses who could use it. What we did, we did from our collective individual experiences.

In most unprepared business cases, a Value Gap existed between expectations of the owner and pricing realities in their industry or market. A small percentage of owners embraced our readiness concept, and we were invited to help as their Value Advisor. Those relationships lasted 1 to 3 years, depending upon the scope of preparation required. Each company had unique needs. We provided insights to influence value and held quarterly conference calls to review internal progress in their journey of preparation. I noticed these owners who adopted the Value-Prep process became educated in and diligently committed to increasing value in their businesses. The outcomes were starting to pay off in higher multiples.

At the same time, I considered how I could transform what we intrinsically knew from our collective experiences to turn it into a process. I posited how businesses whose value was neutral could re-orient and build value with redirection using key questions. I imagined how successful we could be if there were a repeatable process in place to guide any of us! Our collective business experiences provided me with a lens to capture themes. Over time, I captured important Value observations and lessons learned.

What I also observed was that we did not have all the answers. On the contrary, our disciplined question-based approach elicited valuable insight and feedback for the business owner. Our listening, questioning, and eventual guidance provided those owners increased, measurable value by increasing EBITDA, which in turn increased the Fair Market Value of their company. That's when I correlated how meaningful preparation (readiness) could be to a business owner. For an owner who typically has up to 85% of their personal wealth invested and locked inside the business, maximizing life-long business value has rare significance. It also struck me that owners needed to be educated on Value and how to go about building and protecting wealth in their businesses long before considering a sale.

My hypothesis on using business preparation and readiness to improve Value was tested in several live cases as an M&A

advisor. I observed -- *the more prepared a business, the more likely it would be sold with a higher value.* It is said that to be a good teacher, you need to be a good student. Accepting the offer to create and teach my first live course for a national M&A Association in 2019 on *How to Prepare a Business for Sale to Maximize Value*, I researched extensively. The course was designed with the Simplified Value-Prep® process as its core lesson for a specific application: the sale of a business to a third party. Simplified Value-Prep® is the proven process that germinated from my accumulation of collective knowledge when performing M&A work. These firsthand advisory experiences were integrated as a four-step process I branded the COACH Method™ for business readiness.

By design, Simplified Value-Prep® creates a path any business owner can follow. The COACH Method™ (Calculate, Orient, Adapt, CHoose), is Simplified Value-Prep®'s underlying tasks which are designed to be easily followed. In fact, most owners assign the initial tasks to a trusted CFO, Controller, or Executive Assistant to assist them to complete. The owner is reserved for strategic analysis and decision-making with an advisor as a guide. The eureka moment to formalize my *Theory of Readiness™* occurred after teaching my course live and online, with an offer to teach it again in May 2022. The universal purpose of the *Theory of Readiness™* came to me after I completed *Mac & Murphy*, which illustrates Murphy's lack of preparedness as he struggles with a looming crisis, and Mac's wisdom in being prepared when a chance event struck.

Theory of Readiness™ applies to preparing *any business to be in a constant state of readiness for* whatever events may occur, by choice or by chance. It features actionable goals to build value and insulate the business, protecting long-term business wealth.

Theory of Readiness™ is supported anecdotally and quantitatively. By measuring the change in value over a relatively short period of time, an owner sees value build with the leverage of a Multiple. By mitigating risks to reach a readiness state, a prepared value is further protected. That part of the process makes timing irrelevant and de-risks the negative impact of chance events. The underlying process for creating business readiness, Simplified Value-Prep®, supports the *Theory of Readiness*™ by identifying and quantifying Value. At the same time, the process asks questions required to de-risk the business to create valuable options.

Every owner who has avoided a business crisis or catastrophe can appreciate the priceless effect of readiness protection when confronted with a chance negative event. Not only are crises emotionally draining for the entire company, but they are also equally damaging when options are limited, and when confidence in execution is absent. Having peace of mind that the business is in a readiness state provides decision support confidence. It's easier to make the right decision when faced with any creative or critical situation—an acquisition, new investment in product lines, analysis of a competitor's offer to buy you, or when unforeseen chance events portend a crisis. That is why I believe the most important decision you face in business, in our growing world of complexity, is to Value-Prep or not to Value-Prep? By using Simplified Value-Prep® as your tool you can make it EASY to build and protect your business wealth.

GROW CASH & BUILD VALUE!

Today more than ever before, the emphasis in financial management is on growing cash flow and building value. Just ask any banker about the importance of debt service coverage ratios! Every stakeholder with a financial interest is wondering how to mitigate risks and improve cash flow. Simplified Value-Prep® is locked in step with the benefits associated with increasing and protecting cash flow.

From another perspective, business sales and transfers are at a socio-demographic point where there will be fewer and fewer qualified buyers in the future as Baby Boomers transfer $10 Trillion in value to subsequent generations of owners. This will happen in the next 10-12 years. That means only the best-in-class businesses will be attractive to strategic and financial buyers. The sweat equity of the owner will not count for much in the marketplace unless it is backed by a business with recurring revenues and strong cash flow. That's why the single most important financial metric in evaluating the progress of a privately held business is Fair Market Value. By identifying those actions that build and drive value, you will get a much better return when it's time to exit or transfer the business. Simplified Value-Prep® is a unique tool to help any owner see how increasing EBITDA and cash flow converts to increased Value and buyer attractiveness.

HOW MUCH CAN YOU EXPECT IN RETURN?

A specific answer depends upon unique factors about your business that are uncovered during the process and the primary reason to use Simplified Value-Prep®. Generally, the minimum goal of business preparation is to increase EBITDA (Earnings Before Interest Taxes & Depreciation). The calculation is simple. If your business has a Fair Market Value of 4X (known as the Multiple) times EBITDA, and you raise that 4X by 1X to 5X

EBITDA because you are prepared and have things in order to make the business more attractive to the marketplace, you have increased your return by 25%. For example, if your EBITDA is $500,000 @ 4X = $2,000,000 and Value-Prepping yields you an additional $500,000, wouldn't you be pleased? The impacts of Multiple are substantial.

In addition to Simplified Value-Prep® being designed to build value, there is one intrinsic benefit of preparation that protects value. The resultant readiness state is like having built-in "self-insurance" to protect value when faced with sudden events. The self-insurance aspect acts as a decision support tool for strategic decisions. For instance, there may be an acquisition that suddenly appears which would catapult your growth. Unless you have done your Value-Prepping homework, how can you responsibly respond and rapidly purchase another one? Should a crisis occur, knowing what contingencies you have as they relate to the value of your business is critical. Thinking through your contingencies now can keep you ahead of any potential crisis. As a turnaround colleague once asked, "Why would you pay double, triple, or five times more to get out of trouble, when with a small investment of time in strategic plan-ning, you could have avoided trouble altogether?" That same outlook applies to Value-Prepping.

In business, you pay for general, property, casualty, EPLI, medical, life, and disability insurance premiums throughout the life of the business, for any number of potential calamities. Yet, many business owners resist the modest investment of time involved in Value-Prepping their businesses. Agreed. It is much easier to ignore Value-Prepping and do nothing. However, that decision inevitably takes its toll on selling price and limits options during a crisis. So why place that hard-earned value at risk in the first place? With time as your real enemy, having options is priceless. Simplified Value-Prep® allows you the peace of mind to know you've considered the value impact of your strategic decisions regardless of whether it is a crisis event or a golden egg opportunity. Your Simplified Value-Prep® Plan becomes the instrumental decision support tool as your business faces a complex and changing future.

IT'S TIME TO DECIDE.

Timing may or may not be in your favor when it is time to sell or transfer your business. We don't have a crystal ball, nor can we predict the events leading up to a sale, or those that may influence a transaction. However, we can be prepared for the transfer of value that we know with certainty happens with every business. Value-prepping is something we do control. And there's no better time than now to begin the value-prepping process.

The key to being able to take advantage of opportunities that confront the business, or to avoid a catastrophe, is to make timing irrelevant. Simplified Value-Prep® puts you in control. You may be faced with a strategic acquisition and know there's plenty of cash available to do so, or that you are bankable. Or there may be a new product line that demands an initial slug of capital or research & development costs to bring it to commercialization, which catapults you past competitors. Or you may be approached with an opportunity to re-capitalize at a high multiple and take some equity off the table. Whatever the situations you will face, the benefits of value-prepping are significant in context for decision support to make creative and critical decisions in your business.

This is the case for using Simplified Value Prep®. That's why

I believe every business owner needs to consider and answer the question now: To Value-Prep, or not to Value-Prep? I assure you, that answer is the single most influential and important business decision you will ever make.

Make it EASY,

David Wayne Wimer, Founder
value-prep.com

VALUE CONCEPTS & FINANCIAL DEFINITIONS

"Business Value Preparation" is an organizational strategy that emphasizes actions designed to prepare the business and owner to be and remain in a constant 'readiness state', so that at any time, for any purpose, value is optimized, regardless of chance or choice events. Actions underpin a proven process for being organized and prepared, therefore in a constant 'ready' state, regardless of chance or choice events that may occur, thereby protecting business value.

"Certified Business Intermediary" (CBI®) is an experienced business broker who is committed to the highest level of professional development the industry has to offer and has ethical values aligned with the IBBA® standards of professionalism. A CBI® can objectively guide clients through the intricacies of the entire marketing and negotiation process of a business sale, resulting in successful transactions and satisfied clients. Along with having undergone a specialized initial program of detailed training, a CBI is required to earn continuing education credits to maintain the credential.

"Certified Financial Planner" (CFP™) certification is the standard of excellence in financial planning. CFP® professionals meet rigorous education, training, and ethical standards, and are committed to serving their clients' best interests today to prepare them for a more secure tomorrow. They use their knowledge and expertise to construct personalized financial plans that aim to achieve the financial goals of clients. These plans include not only investments but also savings, budget, insurance, and tax strategies.

"Certified Valuation Analyst" (CVA®) is established by the National Association of Certified Valuators and Analysts® (NACVA®), and it is the only valuation credential accredited by the National Commission for Certifying Agencies® (NCCA®), the accreditation body of the Institute for Credentialing Excellence™ (ICE™), and the American National Standards Institute® (ANSI®). The CVA designation is an indication to the business, professional, and legal communities that recipients have met the rigorous standards of professionalism, expertise, objectivity, and integrity in the field of business valuation, financial consulting and litigation, and related consulting disciplines.

"Case-based Learning" is an essential part of business education as it enables students to discover and develop their unique framework for dealing with business problems, using an actual Case Study. The important peculiarity of the business case study is that it introduces a slice of realism into the learning experience. The case study method helps the students in developing wisdom and broadens the scope for knowledge application on a live situation they may encounter in the market.

"Case Study" is the most effective teaching technique of practical application skills in today's business environment. It enables students examining different business situations, in various cultural and economic perspectives, to open their minds by solving problems of a real business situation.

"COACH" is an acronym for the four actions of Business Value

Preparation in the COACH Method™ :

I. Calculate – an Enterprise Value

II. Orient – to the goals & objectives of the owner

III. Adapt – make changes to support goals & objectives

IV. CHoose – evaluate new options

"COACH Method™" is the step-by-step process methodology for Business Value Preparation using the four actions to achieve a constant state of business readiness, prepared for any reason, including chance or choice events.

"COACH Quadrant" is one of the four Action Quadrants in the COACH Method™ . The Quadrants are: Calculate. Orient. Adapt. CHoose.

"Cross-Functional Teams" are a short-term group of people from different areas of the business who come together for specific problem-solving, or continuous improvement. Usually, the team is put in place for rapid change management inside the business with specific objectives to accomplish. The group generally has a leader and a communications path direct to the owner. Team characteristics also include diversity, collaboration, excellent communications skills, the authority to make decisions and a process-orientation.

"EBITDA" is Earnings Before Interest, Taxes, Depreciation & Amortization, and is used in calculating business value. Average EBITDA is the mean of computing several years and dividing by the number of years. Weighted EBITDA is the weighting of more recent years higher than earlier years, giving the benefit of more recent performance to the business value.

"Enterprise Value" (EV) is a measure of a company's total value, often used as a more comprehensive alternative to equity market capitalization. Enterprise value includes in its calculation the market capitalization of a company, but also short-term and long-term debt, as well as any cash on the company's balance sheet.

"Fair Market Value" (FMV) in its simplest sense, is the price an asset would sell for on the open market. FMV has come to represent the price of an asset under the following usual set of conditions: prospective buyers and sellers are reasonably knowledgeable about the asset, behaving in their own best interest, free of undue pressure to trade, and given a reasonable time for completing the transaction. Given these conditions, an asset's FMV should represent an accurate valuation or assessment of its worth.

"Family Office" provides a broad spectrum of private wealth management services to one or a small number of ultra-high-net-worth families. Besides financial services, family offices also offer planning, charitable giving advice, concierge, and other comprehensive services. Single-family offices serve one individual and their family, while multi-family offices serve a few families benefiting from economies of scale.

"FINRA" means the Financial Industry Regulatory Authority, Inc.; (a) "FINRA Board" means the FINRA Board of Governors; (b) "FINRA member" means any broker or dealer admitted to membership in FINRA.

"FINRA Series" administered by FINRA and known as the

general securities representative license. The Series 7 license authorizes an agent to sell virtually any type of individual security, such as preferred stocks, options, bonds, and other individual fixed income investments—plus all forms of packaged products.

"Financial Advisor" is a professional who provides expertise for individual's decisions around money matters, personal finances, and investments called a Personal Financial Plan. Financial advisors may work as independent agents, or they may be employed by a larger financial firm. They are FINRA licensed for the representation of any type of individual security. Also known as Registered Financial Advisors. Unlike stockbrokers, who simply execute orders in the market, registered financial advisors provide guidance and make informed decisions on behalf of their clients.

"Merger & Acquisition Master Intermediary" (M&AMI®) The M&A Source® Merger & Acquisition Master Intermediary® Certification is a proprietary designation that affords professional growth and marketability unlike any other in the M&A profession. This title distinguishes each of the holders as seasoned M&A professionals who have a solid educational background, proven accomplishments in completing deals, and a strong passion for the M&A Source and the M&A profession. The Master designation is the only one to require both educational credits and the successful completion of multiple middle-market transactions.

"Owner's Wish List" is a document that outlines the business owner's goals and objectives during the Orient Quadrant of the

COACH Method™ for Simplified Value-Prep. It addresses what the owner wants from the business long-term. During a negotiation it would address what the owner sees as key deal points to accomplish. Having a written, numbered list assists the owner in clarifying wants and needs and prioritizes the efforts of the lead negotiator.

"Letter of Guidance" is the list of critical items an owner creates in case of emergency (ICE) should the owner be incapacitated. The one-page document includes key professionals such as CPA, Attorney and Advisors of the business, who may be left in charge of the business in the interim period or who may be the family member liaison, a list of passwords and bank accounts which can be referenced to a secure electronic vault, and any specific items that may only be known quickly by an owner.

"Multiple" is applied to a specific financial metric of a company to calculate the business' valuation or assess its reasonability. The most common financial metrics that multiples are applied to include EBITDA, EBIT, Net Earnings, and Revenue. If a multiple is applied to a pre-debt number, like EBITDA, EBIT or Revenue, the resulting valuation is the estimated enterprise value. If the multiple is applied to an after-debt number, such as net earnings, the resulting valuation is the estimated equity value. A multiple is referred to as "4 times", "4x" or "4 turns", as an example, which would refer to EBITDA being multiplied times 4 to yield the estimated valuation of a company.

"Opportunity Analysis" is the list of potential changes in the business to close Value Gaps. Each Opportunity is defined on a spreadsheet by a description of the goal, project leader, team members, and action(s) to be taken, prioritized by the financial return to the business. An owner, sponsoring change, may use the Opportunity Analysis to attack low-hanging fruit, to achieve easy wins building confidence of the cross-collaborative team. Owner(s) can track and measure progress over short, 90-day windows when initiating change.

"Pareto Principal of 80/20" is named after Vilfredo Pareto who in 1906 at the age of 58 observed that 20% of the population owned 80% of the land in Italy. Pareto was an Italian civil engineer, sociologist, economist, political scientist, and philosopher. The 80-20 rule, also known as the Pareto Principle, is an aphorism which asserts that 80% of outcomes (or outputs) result from 20% of all causes (or inputs) for any given event. In the context of value improvement, Pareto is applied as a prioritization tool given that resources are generally finite when making changes in the business. In other words, Pareto gets "more bang for the buck."

"Personal Financial Plan" is a modeling tool designed for managing personal finances. It encompasses budgeting, banking, insurance, mortgages, investments, retirement planning, and tax and estate planning. The model uses current income and expenses at any one point in time to project future needs compared to the needs and desires of the individual or household. The plan includes certain agreed upon assumptions of inflation and growth and the appreciation of assets. The plan is effective as a decision support tool for meeting financial goals, such as income, spending, and overall investing strategies.

"Professional Advisors" in the context of a business, is a profes-

sional who assists the owner of a business with specific expertise. Advisors are generally external professionals such as a
CPA, Tax CPA, Business Attorney, Tax Attorney, Patent Attorney,
Litigation Attorney, Certified Valuation Analyst, Certified Financial Planner, Wealth Advisor, Value Advisor, M&A Advisor, or
any other subject-matter expert utilized as a consultant to the
business owner.

"Readiness State" in the context of Business Value Preparation &
Protection means: At any time, for any reason, the business can
be transferred for maximum value, regardless of choice or
chance events.

"Simplified Value-Prep®" (SVP®) is the registered service mark
for the design of the COACH Method™ , a process for Business
Value Preparation & Protection. SVP is utilized by business
brokers & M&A advisors to prepare a business for sale or
transfer and maximize its value.

"Valuation" is a calculation that depends upon purpose, and is
used to determine a range of Fair Market Value for any business.

"Value" is short for Fair Market Value, the price at which a business would sell given the financial and operating condition of
the business at that point in time, under the conditions of Fair
Market Value.

"Value Advisor" is a person skilled in understanding FMV Valuations for the purposes of business planning, value preparation
& protection. They may or may not be certified as a Valuation
Analyst. The Value Advisor usually depends upon their experi-

ence and knowledge of markets. The Value Advisor may also be known as a Corporate Financial Advisor who works with business owners to understand the big picture of Balance Sheet and Profit & Loss reports, Forecasting, Operating Budgets and Financing strategies employed in the business. Ms. Rahbull and Mr. Hastie are Value Advisors in this story.

"Value Factors Assessment" is a self-assessment with 50+ factors that are rated by the owner to view the business in terms of Value, which leads to discussions of Value Gaps.

"Value Gap Analysis" is the identification of any gap between a) what an owner may perceive as Value, b) what a Fair Market Value (FMV) Valuation is for the business, and c) what the current market may indicate through comparable sales and industry reports, taking into consideration economic climate.

"Value Mindset" is a view on using value in the business as a key performance indicator and standard business tool. It includes teaching value concepts to people in the business who understand drivers of value and detractors of value. Everyone becomes oriented to a value mindset, growth, and risk mitigation in the business.

"Value-Prep Plan" is the outcome of using the Simplified Value-Prep® process for business value preparation and protection. The Value-Prep Plan is managed on Value-Prep.com, a cloud-based, on-line electronic vault to track, store and organize electronic documents. The Value-Prep Plan is confidential, cyber-secure, and meets the requirements of critical privacy standards such as HIPAA & CCPA.

"Value-Prepping" is the act of using Simplified Value-Prep®.

"Wealth Management Advisor" is a high-level professional who manages an affluent client's wealth holistically, typically for one set fee. This service is usually appropriate for wealthy individuals with a broad array of diverse needs.

THE SIMPLIFIED VALUE-PREP® MODEL

The COACH Method™ underpins a proven process for Value-Prepping a business to be in a constant 'readiness' state, regardless of chance or choice events that may occur, thereby protecting business value. More can be learned at Value-Prep.com.

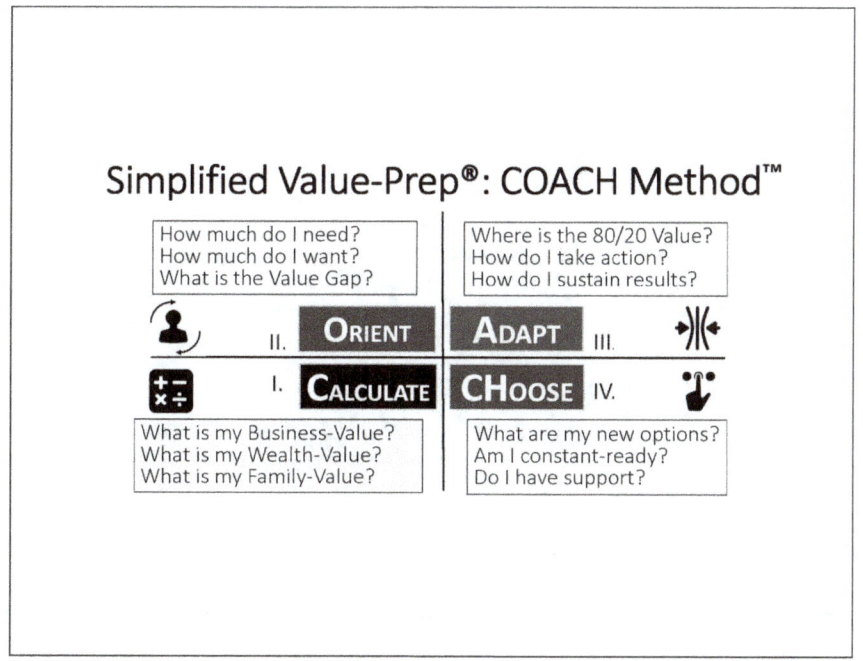

www.ingramcontent.com/pod-product-compliance
Lightning Source LLC
Chambersburg PA
CBHW060332130626
46553CB00003B/991